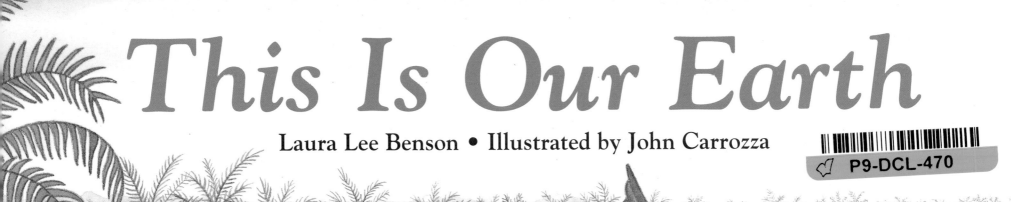

# This Is Our Earth

Laura Lee Benson • Illustrated by John Carrozza

P9-DCL-470

To my parents, Robert and Joyce Benson. — LLB

For Jules, Matthew, and Theo. A special thank you to Anastasia Grantis and Jarad Saunders! — JC

Charlesbridge

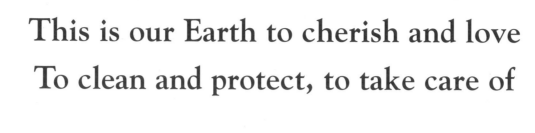

# This is our Earth to cherish and love
## To clean and protect, to take care of

So many people live on Earth! And there are more of us each year. In order for us all to live in a healthy and prosperous way, we must share and carefully protect Earth's natural resources — the air, water, land, and food supplies.

From the mountains so high with their rugged terrain
To the valleys below and the green grassy plain

Located high up in the Rocky Mountains, the Continental Divide is the imaginary line that separates eastern rivers from western rivers. Eastern rivers flow into the Atlantic Ocean or the Gulf of Mexico. Western rivers flow into the Pacific Ocean. No rivers cross the Continental Divide.

# From the tall wooded forests with their towering trees

People benefit from trees in many important ways. Their leaves make oxygen that is a vital ingredient in the air we breathe. The leaves also provide cool shade on hot summer days. Trees play another important role — paper is made from trees!

# To the fish, whales, and dolphins that live in the seas

All animals breathe. Like human beings, whales and dolphins have lungs so they must come to the water's surface to breathe air. Fish breathe underwater by using their gills to filter oxygen from the water.

# From the deserts of sand
# Where the tall cactus grow

Deserts are dry — they receive less than ten inches of rain per year. We may think of deserts as vast stretches of land covered by sand. The majority of the world's deserts are not carpets of sand, but are covered with gravel, stones, and scattered boulders.

# To the cold Arctic north
# With its glaciers and snow

The largest glacier on Earth covers an area of land bigger than the United States. This glacier blankets Antarctica, the continent that lies at Earth's South Pole. The ice and snow are so deep that only the mountaintops are not covered by this mighty glacier.

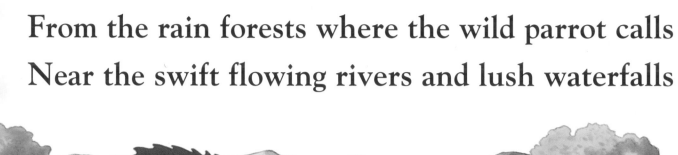

From the rain forests where the wild parrot calls
Near the swift flowing rivers and lush waterfalls

The greatest variety of plants and animals found anywhere on Earth is in rain forests. Living conditions are ideal for plants and animals because there's an abundance of sunlight, rain, and food. Rain forests receive 160 to 400 inches of rain per year! Do you remember how much rain a desert receives?

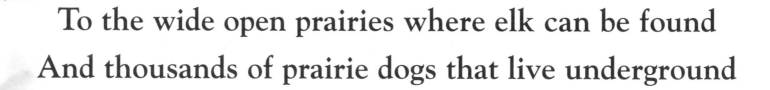

To the wide open prairies where elk can be found
And thousands of prairie dogs that live underground

The prairie is sometimes described as a sea of grass. There are more grasses than any other form of plant life on the rolling prairie lands. Big bluestem is a species of prairie grass that grows six feet tall. That's taller than most people!

From the shimmering lakes where flocks of geese swim
And the blue jay keeps watch from a lofty tree limb

When birds fly south every year as the weather turns cold, they follow the same flyways — paths in the sky. No one knows for certain how birds find their way, but we think they use the sun and stars, and land forms like coasts, rivers, and mountains to guide them on their long journey.

# To the farms in the country
# Where cows graze on hay

Most dairy farms have cows to produce milk, but some have buffalos, goats, or sheep instead. One milk cow can give more than a thousand gallons of milk per year. That's 44 glasses of milk every day!

# And the parks in the cities where children play.

The Boston Common, a famous city park, became America's first public park in 1634. But it started out as a cow pasture! Yellowstone National Park in Wyoming was the world's first national park, established in 1872.

So take a good look
And I think you will find

Look closely at sand — it is really tiny pieces of rock. Most sand is light brown, but there is white sand in Florida and green sand in Hawaii. In other places you can find beaches that have black, volcanic sand.

That this beautiful Earth

Is one of a kind.

The Earth has many natural wonders such as the Grand Canyon in Arizona. At one place, the Grand Canyon is 5,500 feet deep. That is deep enough to hold the world's four tallest buildings stacked one on top of the other!

Let's do our share to lend a hand
To preserve all we have in this wonderful land.

Each of us must help in our own way, each day, to keep the land we live on clean and beautiful. Please throw litter in the trash can. Whenever possible, recycle glass, paper, metal, and plastic. Learn what else you can do to help!

This is our Earth to cherish and love
To clean and protect from below and above.

Seen from outer space, Earth looks blue and white. The blue is the ocean water and the white, swirls of clouds. How beautiful and wonderful this place we call home. Let's share it and take care of it — together we will protect Earth from harm.

# THIS IS OUR EARTH

This is our Earth to cher-ish and love to clean and pro-tect to take care of

From the moun-tains so high with their rug-ged ter-rain, to the val-leys be-low

and the green gras-sy plain. This is our Earth. This is our Earth.

**I**

This is our Earth to cherish and love
To clean and protect, to take care of
From the mountains so high with their rugged terrain
To the valleys below and the green grassy plain,
This is our Earth.

**II**

From the tall wooded forests with their towering trees
To the fish, whales, and dolphins that live in the seas
From the deserts of sand where the tall cactus grow
To the cold Arctic north with its glaciers and snow,
This is our Earth.

**III**

From the rain forests where the wild parrot calls
Near the swift flowing rivers and lush waterfalls
To the wide open prairies where elk can be found
And thousands of prairie dogs that live underground,
This is our Earth.

**IV**

From the shimmering lakes where flocks of geese swim
And the blue jay keeps watch from a lofty tree limb
To the farms in the country where cows graze on hay
And the parks in the cities where children play,
This is our Earth.

**V**

So take a good look and I think you will find
That this beautiful Earth is one of a kind.
Let's do our share to lend a hand
To preserve all we have in this wonderful land,
This is our Earth.

**VI**

This is our Earth to cherish and love
To clean and protect, to take care of
This is our Earth to cherish and love
To clean and protect from below and above,
This is our Earth.

Published by Charlesbridge Publishing • 85 Main Street, Watertown, MA 02472 • (617) 926-0329 • www.charlesbridge.com

Printed in the United States of America
(sc) 10  9  8  7
(hc) 10  9  8  7  6  5  4  3  2

**Library of Congress Cataloging-in-Publication Data**
Available upon request

ISBN 0-88106-838-1 (softcover)
ISBN 0-88106-839-X (reinforced for library use)